Taking the Tests

Your child should record their answers in the Answer Sheets booklet provided – not in the test booklet. Answer Sheets are provided for all three tests in this pack.

The actual 11+ test will be marked by a computer, but you will need to score the practice tests yourself using the Answer Key in this booklet. It is important for your child to learn how to use the Answer Sheets properly, in preparation for the real test: they should record an answer in the appropriate box by drawing a clear line through it with a pencil. Mistakes should be rubbed out carefully and **not** crossed out, since in the actual test this would not be recorded correctly by the computer. You can ignore the boxes at the top marked 'Pupil Number', 'School Number' and 'Date of Birth'. These need to be filled in only for the actual test. By encountering these features now, your child will be more familiar with the style of the actual 11+ paper when they take the test.

Timing a Test

It is useful for your child to practise taking tests under timed conditions. Allow them 50 minutes for a test, but do not start timing until they have read all the instructions and/or filled in all the details at the top of the Answer Sheet.

If they have not finished at the end of 50 minutes, draw a line underneath the question they are on, or draw a ring around its number, and then let them carry on. When you mark the test, you will be able to see how many questions your child got right in the allocated time and how many questions overall. This will give you a good indication of whether they need to develop their speed and/or work more accurately.

Marking and Feedback

The answers are provided on pages 4 – 6. Only these answers are allowed. One mark should be given for each correct answer – do not allow half marks or 'the benefit of the doubt'. Do not deduct marks for wrong answers.

The results may suggest that more practice is needed. Always try to be positive and encouraging. Talk through the mistakes your child has made in a constructive way. Work out together how to get the right answer.

Answer Key

Question	Answer	Question	Answer	Question	Answer
1	that all	26	mat	56	B
2	This item	27	costs		
3	were stuck	28	path	57	hope, less
4	winter months.	29	lend	58	data, base
5	than dogs.	30	fail	59	over, take
6	through open	31	hilt	60	perm, it
				61	act, or
7	A	32	PAR	62	he, art
8	E	33	ICE		
9	E	34	MEN	63	scent
10	B	35	RID	64	waste
11	B	36	KEY	65	plain
12	C	37	TEA	66	outstanding
				67	order
13	u	38	IR	68	kind
14	o	39	HK		
15	t	40	GK	69	canal, tarmac
16	a	41	EG	70	carpet, curtain
17	c	42	GH	71	milk, desert
18	r	43	NT	72	racket, stadium
				73	spoon, wheel
19	weight, length	44	harm, hurt	74	head, car
20	take, give	45	soften, melt		
21	below, above	46	skilful, able	75	ODPE
22	buckle, collar	47	echo, repeat	76	XKT
23	up, down	48	raise, elevate	77	PINK
24	weak, timid	49	customer, client	78	HMQRDYNJ
				79	GRASS
25	Lucy	50	37	80	WKRPNT
		51	49		
		52	240		
		53	67		
		54	25		
		55	62		

Notes and Answers for Parents

Verbal Reasoning
Pack 1

GL Assessment®

11+ Practice Papers

Introduction

About the Tests

These tests are designed to give your child practice in sitting a formal type of examination before they take the actual 11+ test.

The papers are presented in a very similar way to many of the test papers used for selection at 11+, and the questions represent the type of questions used, although they may not be exactly the same level of difficulty. Therefore, your child's scores on these tests will not necessarily be a direct indication of their likely score on an actual 11+ test. Furthermore, the pass marks for the actual test will depend, to some extent, on the overall standard of the candidates.

Preparation for Testing

Give your child the test at an appropriate time, when they are both physically and mentally alert. Choose a suitable area for them to work in – make sure they can work comfortably and are free from any distractions.

Before your child takes a practice test, discuss with them the reasons why they are doing the test. Also, explain that they might find some of the questions difficult, but that they should work as quickly and as carefully as they can. If they get stuck on a question, they should not waste too much time on it but move on to the next one. If they have time left at the end, they can go back to it then.

Answer Key

Question	Answer	Question	Answer	Question	Answer
1	h	26	hear	56	D
2	t	27	teams		
3	g	28	near	57	library, bank
4	y	29	train	58	late, start
5	t	30	name	59	feet, hands
6	k	31	feel	60	is, see
				61	hurricane, downpour
7	86	32	KM	62	help, delay
8	17	33	EG		
9	41	34	HJ	63	XY
10	49	35	SR	64	NL
11	8	36	VX	65	WY
12	61	37	MK	66	KL
				67	WD
13	rain, coat	38	ALL	68	WX
14	had, dock	39	PAL		
15	hope, less	40	PIN	69	little, small
16	temp, late	41	TEE	70	error, mistake
17	reap, pear	42	LIE	71	cot, cradle
18	do, nation	43	OUR	72	quick, rapid
				73	eat, feed
19	china, pottery	44	t	74	above, over
20	handle, hand	45	l		
21	sweet, soft	46	i	75	NEED
22	pour, tip	47	d	76	NOTE
23	arms, legs	48	a	77	6183
24	around, across	49	r	78	5132
				79	5345
25	B	50	B	80	3442
		51	E		
		52	C		
		53	E		
		54	C		
		55	D		

Answer Key

Practice Paper 3

Question	Answer	Question	Answer	Question	Answer
1	girl ate	26	tape	56	D
2	area all	27	the		
3	bottles should	28	loop	57	plant, knife
4	get ripe	29	tail	58	sky, sea
5	is hotter	30	alert	59	paper, glass
6	hurt his	31	spat	60	generous, kind
				61	front, back
7	81	32	BIN	62	month, day
8	2	33	YJKVG		
9	10	34	BIDFSBG	63	l
10	7	35	SPROUTS	64	r
11	2	36	SPOT	65	n
12	32	37	NBPUA	66	e
				67	s
13	work, labour	38	CAR	68	i
14	bowl, dish	39	OUT		
15	stone, rock	40	ARE	69	QR
16	bucket, pail	41	RAT	70	TS
17	funny, witty	42	ONE	71	UX
18	flower, blossom	43	OLD	72	HE
				73	OP
19	over, under	44	back, ground	74	XB
20	joy, sad	45	under, wear		
21	feet, head	46	green, house	75	m
22	garden, lawn	47	in, form	76	p
23	lightning, thunder	48	bar, gain	77	e
24	because, beware	49	man, age	78	w
				79	k
25	Beth	50	48	80	y
		51	23		
		52	32		
		53	17		
		54	147		
		55	25		

Published by GL Assessment, 1st Floor, Vantage London, Great West Road, Brentford TW8 9AG.

Designed and typeset by Peter Francis.

Code 6801 033
1(11.18) PF

Answer Sheets

Verbal Reasoning
Practice Papers 1–3

This booklet contains the answer sheets needed for Verbal Reasoning Practice Papers 1–3.

Please make sure you use the correct answer sheet for the test being taken, following the title at the top of each page.

The following answer sheets are included:

Verbal Reasoning Practice Paper 1
Verbal Reasoning Practice Paper 2
Verbal Reasoning Practice Paper 3

GL Assessment®

Published by GL Assessment, 1st Floor, Vantage London, Great West Road, Brentford TW8 9AG.

Designed and typeset by Peter Francis.

Code 6801 034
1(11.18) PF

VERBAL REASONING PRACTICE PAPER 1

Pupil's Name		DATE OF TEST
School Name		Day / Month / Year

UNIQUE PUPIL NUMBER	SCHOOL NUMBER	DATE OF BIRTH
		Day / Month / Year

Please mark boxes with a thin horizontal line like this ▬.

EXAMPLE
The film ☐
film ended ▬
ended happily ☐
happily after ☐
after all. ☐

1
They saw ☐
saw that ☐
that all ☐
all the ☐
the cake ☐

2
This item ☐
item is ☐
is out ☐
out of ☐
of stock. ☐

3
Posters were ☐
were stuck ☐
stuck on ☐
on the ☐
the bedroom ☐

4
School began ☐
began later ☐
later during ☐
during winter ☐
winter months. ☐

5
Cats have ☐
have better ☐
better eyesight ☐
eyesight than ☐
than dogs. ☐

6
Wasps fly ☐
fly in ☐
in through ☐
through open ☐
open windows. ☐

EXAMPLE
A ☐
B ☐
C ☐
D ▬
E ☐

7
A ☐
B ☐
C ☐
D ☐
E ☐

8
A ☐
B ☐
C ☐
D ☐
E ☐

9
A ☐
B ☐
C ☐
D ☐
E ☐

10
A ☐
B ☐
C ☐
D ☐
E ☐

11
A ☐
B ☐
C ☐
D ☐
E ☐

12
A ☐
B ☐
C ☐
D ☐
E ☐

EXAMPLE
p ☐
o ☐
u ▬
n ☐
d ☐

13
c ☐
o ☐
u ☐
l ☐
d ☐

14
f ☐
l ☐
o ☐
a ☐
t ☐

15
s ☐
t ☐
i ☐
c ☐
k ☐

16
g ☐
r ☐
a ☐
i ☐
n ☐

17
m ☐
i ☐
n ☐
c ☐
e ☐

18
r ☐
e ☐
a ☐
c ☐
h ☐

EXAMPLE
small ▬   apple ☐
orange ☐   red ▬
colour ☐   narrow ▬

19
fins ☐   tail ☐
pounds ☐   length ☐
weight ☐   ounces ☐

20
take ☐   give ☐
crime ☐   victim ☐
money ☐   blood ☐

21
below ☐   steep ☐
country ☐   above ☐
green ☐   jagged ☐

22
leather ☐   collar ☐
buckle ☐   trousers ☐
laces ☐   waistcoat ☐

23
high ☐   down ☐
walk ☐   move ☐
up ☐   hunch ☐

24
weak ☐   carry ☐
great ☐   timid ☐
lift ☐   grand ☐

25
Katie ☐
Adam ☐
Lucy ☐
Ranjit ☐
Mark ☐

EXAMPLE
bud ▬
beg ☐
dug ☐
bed ☐
wed ☐

26
ham ☐
hat ☐
mad ☐
sat ☐
mat ☐

27
casts ☐
tasks ☐
stack ☐
facts ☐
costs ☐

28
that ☐
real ☐
path ☐
reap ☐
hats ☐

29
rend ☐
lend ☐
lent ☐
rate ☐
land ☐

30
lets ☐
fame ☐
mail ☐
flea ☐
fail ☐

31
hair ☐
hill ☐
hail ☐
halt ☐
hilt ☐

EXAMPLE
LAD ☐
LAW ▬
HAD ☐
RAW ☐
RED ☐

32
HAM ☐
HOP ☐
LAP ☐
PAR ☐
TAN ☐

33
EAT ☐
ANT ☐
ICE ☐
ALL ☐
IMP ☐

34
MAN ☐
WIN ☐
MEN ☐
MEW ☐
WAY ☐

35
RUN ☐
AND ☐
LID ☐
ASK ☐
RID ☐

36
KEY ☐
CAR ☐
PIN ☐
SET ☐
ROD ☐

37
PAL ☐
OAK ☐
TEA ☐
ALE ☐
TAR ☐

11+VR-1   **PLEASE TURN OVER**

EXAMPLE
RT ☐
SR ☐
ST ☐
RS ▬
QR ☐

38
IS ☐
IT ☐
GT ☐
IR ☐
JQ ☐

39
HK ☐
GJ ☐
HL ☐
FI ☐
GD ☐

40
GK ☐
GI ☐
HL ☐
FJ ☐
FK ☐

41
GE ☐
DF ☐
EG ☐
GI ☐
CE ☐

42
HI ☐
HG ☐
IJ ☐
GH ☐
FG ☐

43
MT ☐
NQ ☐
NT ☐
QT ☐
OT ☐

EXAMPLE
office ☐   work ☐
shop ☐   begin ▬
start ▬   end ☐

44
game ☐   play ☐
trick ☐   hurt ☐
harm ☐   chess ☐

45
liquid ☐   solid ☐
bend ☐   set ☐
soften ☐   melt ☐

46
sad ☐   concerned ☐
skilful ☐   able ☐
happy ☐   lucky ☐

47
answer ☐   hollow ☐
echo ☐   call ☐
pretend ☐   repeat ☐

48
raise ☐   high ☐
level ☐   elevate ☐
step ☐   lower ☐

49
flight ☐   client ☐
customer ☐   tourist ☐
collect ☐   expensive ☐

EXAMPLE
16 ☐
11 ☐
10 ▬
9 ☐
12 ☐

50
36 ☐
37 ☐
33 ☐
39 ☐
35 ☐

51
43 ☐
35 ☐
49 ☐
51 ☐
37 ☐

52
234 ☐
240 ☐
192 ☐
196 ☐
220 ☐

53
53 ☐
66 ☐
51 ☐
67 ☐
54 ☐

54
17 ☐
21 ☐
22 ☐
24 ☐
25 ☐

55
60 ☐
46 ☐
44 ☐
62 ☐
38 ☐

56
A ☐
B ☐
C ☐
D ☐
E ☐

EXAMPLE
out ▬   bite ☐
by ☐   like ☐
open ☐   side ▬

57
fast ☐   like ☐
have ☐   ping ☐
hope ☐   less ☐

58
ball ☐   bat ☐
table ☐   base ☐
data ☐   basket ☐

59
pass ☐   tall ☐
time ☐   by ☐
over ☐   take ☐

60
perm ☐   at ☐
with ☐   on ☐
look ☐   it ☐

61
imp ☐   age ☐
old ☐   in ☐
act ☐   or ☐

62
he ☐   low ☐
lie ☐   able ☐
lost ☐   art ☐

EXAMPLE
ball ☐
dirt ☐
plant ☐
earth ▬
universe ☐

63
path ☐
scent ☐
perfume ☐
way ☐
odour ☐

64
corrupt ☐
break ☐
rubbish ☐
scrap ☐
waste ☐

65
unmistakable ☐
unornamented ☐
unpatterned ☐
plain ☐
obvious ☐

66
oustanding ☐
extra ☐
senior ☐
surplus ☐
prime ☐

67
ranked ☐
instruct ☐
demand ☐
tidy ☐
order ☐

68
class ☐
pleasant ☐
variety ☐
kind ☐
nice ☐

EXAMPLE
black ☐
mouse ▬
red ☐
green ☐
hut ▬

69
ship ☐
train ☐
canal ☐
tarmac ☐
bus ☐

70
carpet ☐
curtain ☐
blanket ☐
pillow ☐
sheet ☐

71
milk ☐
desert ☐
camel ☐
zebra ☐
cat ☐

72
tennis ☐
racket ☐
rounders ☐
stadium ☐
football ☐

73
spoon ☐
rake ☐
fork ☐
wheel ☐
spade ☐

74
beret ☐
head ☐
cap ☐
bonnet ☐
car ☐

EXAMPLE
STU ☐
SND ▬
UPF ☐
SRQ ☐
SNE ☐

75
NCPE ☐
ODPE ☐
IXJY ☐
NCOD ☐
ODQF ☐

76
FSB ☐
XJS ☐
FTA ☐
YLU ☐
XKT ☐

77
PEAR ☐
PLUM ☐
PINK ☐
PALE ☐
PUCE ☐

78
HMQRDYNJ ☐
HQQVZCJN ☐
GPPUZCJN ☐
HQQVDCNN ☐
GNPSZCJN ☐

79
BRASS ☐
GRASS ☐
GREEN ☐
GROWS ☐
STAFF ☐

80
WJPMJO ☐
WHPKJO ☐
WHNKHM ☐
WKPNJP ☐
WKRPNT ☐

END OF TEST

Pupil's Name		DATE OF TEST		
School Name		Day	Month	Year

UNIQUE PUPIL NUMBER	SCHOOL NUMBER	DATE OF BIRTH		
		Day	Month	Year

Please mark boxes with a thin horizontal line like this ▬.

EXAMPLE
- p
- n
- f
- t ▬
- c

1
- p
- h
- e
- s
- k

2
- d
- a
- t
- b
- w

3
- t
- n
- g
- s
- p

4
- p
- d
- b
- s
- y

5
- c
- y
- t
- d
- g

6
- c
- m
- s
- n
- k

EXAMPLE
- 3
- 4
- 6
- 8 ▬
- 10

7
- 83
- 84
- 85
- 86
- 87

8
- 17
- 21
- 34
- 39
- 41

9
- 29
- 35
- 37
- 38
- 41

10
- 8
- 35
- 39
- 47
- 49

11
- 7
- 8
- 9
- 11
- 12

12
- 59
- 60
- 61
- 62
- 63

EXAMPLE
- out ▬ bite
- by like
- open side ▬

13
- in coat
- rain fell
- hover croft

14
- door lock
- bad dock
- had ship

15
- rope sat
- hope tie
- car less

16
- in late
- out down
- temp slide

17
- ape pear
- reap wine
- grape ate

18
- combine state
- share nation
- do red

EXAMPLE
- black
- mouse ▬
- red
- green
- hut ▬

19
- mug
- china
- cup
- pottery
- beaker

20
- handle
- hammer
- chisel
- hand
- saw

21
- taste
- sweet
- touch
- soft
- see

22
- river
- stream
- pour
- tip
- brook

23
- eyes
- ears
- arms
- nose
- legs

24
- around
- long
- tall
- wide
- across

25
- A
- B
- C
- D
- E

EXAMPLE
- bud ▬
- beg
- dug
- bed
- wed

26
- tear
- hear
- went
- race
- hare

27
- tears
- steam
- pears
- meats
- teams

28
- pear
- nape
- dear
- pans
- near

29
- trial
- trail
- train
- paint
- plain

30
- mean
- name
- same
- nose
- sane

31
- flee
- blow
- heel
- blew
- feel

EXAMPLE
- GP
- GO ▬
- HO
- GR
- GQ

32
- KM
- KO
- MO
- OM
- KN

33
- EG
- EF
- FG
- FF
- FH

34
- JG
- HI
- JH
- HK
- HJ

35
- SR
- JK
- RQ
- RS
- IJ

36
- WX
- WY
- VW
- VX
- WV

37
- MK
- PR
- MJ
- PS
- ML

EXAMPLE
- LAD ☐
- LAW ▬
- HAD ☐
- RAW ☐
- RED ☐

38
- ALL ☐
- RYE ☐
- ALE ☐
- AWL ☐
- HAS ☐

39
- ARE ☐
- AWE ☐
- ORE ☐
- PAL ☐
- PEA ☐

40
- ELF ☐
- PIT ☐
- PIN ☐
- CAN ☐
- TON ☐

41
- TOP ☐
- ARK ☐
- ART ☐
- TEE ☐
- TEA ☐

42
- LOW ☐
- LIE ☐
- LAY ☐
- RAG ☐
- RAY ☐

43
- ACE ☐
- EEL ☐
- ALL ☐
- OWE ☐
- OUR ☐

EXAMPLE
- p ☐
- o ☐
- u ▬
- n ☐
- d ☐

44
- j ☐
- o ☐
- i ☐
- n ☐
- t ☐

45
- h ☐
- a ☐
- l ☐
- v ☐
- e ☐

46
- b ☐
- r ☐
- a ☐
- i ☐
- n ☐

47
- d ☐
- r ☐
- i ☐
- n ☐
- k ☐

48
- c ☐
- h ☐
- a ☐
- i ☐
- n ☐

49
- h ☐
- o ☐
- r ☐
- s ☐
- e ☐

EXAMPLE
- A ☐
- B ☐
- C ☐
- D ▬
- E ☐

50
- A ☐
- B ☐
- C ☐
- D ☐
- E ☐

51
- A ☐
- B ☐
- C ☐
- D ☐
- E ☐

52
- A ☐
- B ☐
- C ☐
- D ☐
- E ☐

53
- A ☐
- B ☐
- C ☐
- D ☐
- E ☐

54
- A ☐
- B ☐
- C ☐
- D ☐
- E ☐

55
- A ☐
- B ☐
- C ☐
- D ☐
- E ☐

56
- A ☐
- B ☐
- C ☐
- D ☐
- E ☐

EXAMPLE
- small ▬
- orange ☐
- colour ☐
- apple ☐
- red ☐
- narrow ▬

57
- library ☐
- leaf ☐
- tree ☐
- paper ☐
- bank ☐
- pig ☐

58
- dawn ☐
- late ☐
- hour ☐
- bus ☐
- queue ☐
- start ☐

59
- mouth ☐
- feet ☐
- month ☐
- eyes ☐
- hands ☐
- time ☐

60
- is ☐
- will ☐
- not ☐
- hammer ☐
- lake ☐
- see ☐

61
- turn ☐
- hurricane ☐
- tree ☐
- downpour ☐
- umbrella ☐
- queen ☐

62
- help ☐
- stock ☐
- block ☐
- falter ☐
- fail ☐
- delay ☐

EXAMPLE
- RT ☐
- SR ☐
- ST ☐
- RS ▬
- QR ☐

63
- HI ☐
- MN ☐
- XY ☐
- YZ ☐
- TU ☐

64
- ML ☐
- ON ☐
- KJ ☐
- LK ☐
- NL ☐

65
- IK ☐
- OQ ☐
- UW ☐
- XZ ☐
- WY ☐

66
- FG ☐
- IJ ☐
- KL ☐
- NO ☐
- QR ☐

67
- TE ☐
- UE ☐
- WD ☐
- WE ☐
- VG ☐

68
- KL ☐
- EF ☐
- XY ☐
- WX ☐
- RS ☐

EXAMPLE
- office ☐
- shop ☐
- start ▬
- work ☐
- begin ▬
- end ☐

69
- little ☐
- pretty ☐
- cuddle ☐
- small ☐
- sweet ☐
- nice ☐

70
- idea ☐
- error ☐
- accurate ☐
- mistake ☐
- joke ☐
- fool ☐

71
- bib ☐
- cot ☐
- rattle ☐
- sleep ☐
- baby ☐
- cradle ☐

72
- quick ☐
- slow ☐
- idle ☐
- rapid ☐
- race ☐
- arena ☐

73
- bread ☐
- butter ☐
- eat ☐
- peas ☐
- dinner ☐
- feed ☐

74
- high ☐
- above ☐
- apex ☐
- over ☐
- inside ☐
- under ☐

75
- NEED ☐
- SOOT ☐
- SEED ☐
- TOON ☐
- SOON ☐

76
- DOTE ☐
- DATE ☐
- NODE ☐
- NOSE ☐
- NOTE ☐

77
- 6137 ☐
- 3467 ☐
- 7384 ☐
- 6183 ☐
- 7183 ☐

78
- 3145 ☐
- 5132 ☐
- 5432 ☐
- 2135 ☐
- 2315 ☐

79
- 5435 ☐
- 2312 ☐
- 2412 ☐
- 2342 ☐
- 5345 ☐

80
- 2113 ☐
- 3445 ☐
- 3442 ☐
- 2334 ☐
- 1334 ☐

END OF TEST

VERBAL REASONING PRACTICE PAPER 3

Pupil's Name		DATE OF TEST		
School Name		Day	Month	Year

UNIQUE PUPIL NUMBER	SCHOOL NUMBER	DATE OF BIRTH		
		Day	Month	Year

Please mark boxes with a thin horizontal line like this ▭.

EXAMPLE
The film ▭
film ended ▬
ended happily ▭
happily after ▭
after all. ▭

1
The girl ▭
girl ate ▭
ate the ▭
the sponge ▭
sponge cake. ▭

2
Soon they ▭
are all ▭
all going ▭
going on ▭
on holiday. ▭

3
Glass bottles ▭
bottles should ▭
should be ▭
be kept ▭
kept upright. ▭

4
We get ▭
get ripe ▭
ripe apples ▭
apples in ▭
in October. ▭

5
My drink ▭
drink is ▭
is hotter ▭
hotter than ▭
than yours. ▭

6
He had ▭
had hurt ▭
hurt his ▭
his knee ▭
knee badly. ▭

EXAMPLE
1 ▭
2 ▬
3 ▭
4 ▭
5 ▭

7
79 ▭
80 ▭
81 ▭
82 ▭
83 ▭

8
2 ▭
3 ▭
4 ▭
6 ▭
8 ▭

9
7 ▭
8 ▭
9 ▭
10 ▭
11 ▭

10
5 ▭
6 ▭
7 ▭
8 ▭
9 ▭

11
2 ▭
3 ▭
4 ▭
5 ▭
6 ▭

12
12 ▭
16 ▭
24 ▭
30 ▭
32 ▭

EXAMPLE
office ▭   work ▭
shop ▭   begin ▬
start ▬   end ▭

13
work ▭   labour ▭
type ▭   plan ▭
succeed ▭ office ▭

14
soup ▭   bread ▭
fork ▭   dish ▭
bowl ▭   knife ▭

15
stone ▭   hill ▭
sea ▭   rock ▭
beach ▭   grass ▭

16
sand ▭   garden ▭
bucket ▭   spade ▭
water ▭   pail ▭

17
circus ▭   game ▭
funny ▭   clown ▭
laugh ▭   witty ▭

18
flower ▭   spring ▭
tree ▭   blossom ▭
leaf ▭   grass ▭

EXAMPLE
black ▭
mouse ▬
red ▭
green ▭
hut ▬

19
over ▭
under ▭
cricket ▭
tennis ▭
badminton ▭

20
joy ▭
laugh ▭
cry ▭
sad ▭
scream ▭

21
hat ▭
feet ▭
coat ▭
head ▭
shoes ▭

22
bathroom ▭
kitchen ▭
garden ▭
bedroom ▭
lawn ▭

23
lightning ▭
thunder ▭
hail ▭
sleet ▭
snow ▭

24
beneath ▭
because ▭
beware ▭
behind ▭
between ▭

25
Malcolm ▭
Mohammed ▭
Beth ▭
Sally ▭
Robin ▭

EXAMPLE
bud ▬
beg ▭
dug ▭
bed ▭
wed ▭

26
tale ▭
bale ▭
base ▭
tape ▭
peat ▭

27
the ▭
tea ▭
sat ▭
set ▭
hat ▭

28
lord ▭
door ▭
prod ▭
loop ▭
pool ▭

29
tail ▭
tile ▭
last ▭
lost ▭
tale ▭

30
reads ▭
laird ▭
deals ▭
alert ▭
leads ▭

31
spot ▭
step ▭
stop ▭
eats ▭
spat ▭

EXAMPLE
STU ▭
SND ▬
UPF ▭
SRQ ▭
SNE ▭

32
HIT ▭
HOT ▭
HOG ▭
BIN ▭
BIT ▭

33
YJKVG ▭
UFGRC ▭
ZKLWH ▭
ZJKWG ▭
YJLVG ▭

34
BGDDSZG ▭
BIDFSBG ▭
DIFFUZI ▭
DGFDUZI ▭
EJGGVCJ ▭

35
SAUSAGE ▭
FEEDING ▭
SPROUTS ▭
PUDDING ▭
LASAGNE ▭

36
EELS ▭
SPOT ▭
POOL ▭
POND ▭
SOFT ▭

37
NYQSY ▭
NXPUB ▭
NBQUY ▭
RZVSI ▭
NBPUA ▭

11+VR-3   **PLEASE TURN OVER**

EXAMPLE
- LAD ☐
- LAW ▬
- HAD ☐
- RAW ☐
- RED ☐

38
- COT ☐
- CAN ☐
- TAR ☐
- HAT ☐
- CAR ☐

39
- PAR ☐
- COT ☐
- OUT ☐
- ARE ☐
- OUR ☐

40
- ATE ☐
- AIR ☐
- ARE ☐
- OUT ☐
- OWL ☐

41
- HAT ☐
- HIM ☐
- RIM ☐
- RAT ☐
- ROT ☐

42
- APE ☐
- OWN ☐
- ONE ☐
- ARE ☐
- WON ☐

43
- RUN ☐
- OLD ☐
- OWL ☐
- ROC ☐
- AIR ☐

EXAMPLE
- out ▬   bite ☐
- by ☐   like ☐
- open ☐   side ▬

44
- back ☐   pane ☐
- four ☐   ground ☐
- front ☐   under ☐

45
- ear ☐   grind ☐
- are ☐   were ☐
- under ☐   wear ☐

46
- ever ☐   house ☐
- green ☐   moor ☐
- red ☐   dye ☐

47
- top ☐   form ☐
- in ☐   shape ☐
- out ☐   shop ☐

48
- win ☐   rose ☐
- red ☐   doe ☐
- bar ☐   gain ☐

49
- man ☐   fell ☐
- boy ☐   age ☐
- say ☐   here ☐

EXAMPLE
- 16 ☐
- 11 ☐
- 10 ▬
- 9 ☐
- 12 ☐

50
- 64 ☐
- 48 ☐
- 12 ☐
- 4 ☐
- 16 ☐

51
- 22 ☐
- 23 ☐
- 25 ☐
- 29 ☐
- 27 ☐

52
- 32 ☐
- 42 ☐
- 40 ☐
- 30 ☐
- 33 ☐

53
- 20 ☐
- 19 ☐
- 15 ☐
- 17 ☐
- 21 ☐

54
- 57 ☐
- 113 ☐
- 101 ☐
- 147 ☐
- 99 ☐

55
- 50 ☐
- 20 ☐
- 42 ☐
- 25 ☐
- 39 ☐

56
- A ☐
- B ☐
- C ☐
- D ☐
- E ☐

EXAMPLE
- small ▬   apple ☐
- orange ☐   red ☐
- colour ☐   narrow ▬

57
- plant ☐   knife ☐
- green ☐   sharp ☐
- live ☐   ice ☐

58
- distant ☐ swim ☐
- fly ☐   sea ☐
- sky ☐   near ☐

59
- writing ☐ door ☐
- novel ☐   house ☐
- paper ☐   glass ☐

60
- tight ☐   type ☐
- crab ☐   kind ☐
- generous ☐ child ☐

61
- ground ☐   back ☐
- front ☐   leg ☐
- head ☐   air ☐

62
- month ☐   end ☐
- might ☐   day ☐
- season ☐   Thursday ☐

EXAMPLE
- p ☐
- o ☐
- u ▬
- n ☐
- d ☐

63
- p ☐
- l ☐
- a ☐
- n ☐
- t ☐

64
- b ☐
- r ☐
- u ☐
- s ☐
- h ☐

65
- p ☐
- r ☐
- o ☐
- v ☐
- n ☐

66
- c ☐
- h ☐
- e ☐
- a ☐
- p ☐

67
- h ☐
- o ☐
- s ☐
- t ☐
- e ☐

68
- i ☐
- r ☐
- a ☐
- t ☐
- e ☐

EXAMPLE
- RT ☐
- SR ☐
- ST ☐
- RS ▬
- QR ☐

69
- AB ☐
- EF ☐
- TU ☐
- ST ☐
- QR ☐

70
- NM ☐
- PO ☐
- RQ ☐
- TS ☐
- TR ☐

71
- KJ ☐
- ON ☐
- UW ☐
- UX ☐
- XZ ☐

72
- HG ☐
- JH ☐
- HE ☐
- EB ☐
- NL ☐

73
- RS ☐
- PQ ☐
- NO ☐
- OP ☐
- ST ☐

74
- YB ☐
- XB ☐
- YA ☐
- XA ☐
- AY ☐

EXAMPLE
- p ☐
- n ☐
- f ☐
- t ▬
- c ☐

75
- t ☐
- g ☐
- l ☐
- m ☐
- b ☐

76
- t ☐
- d ☐
- m ☐
- r ☐
- p ☐

77
- s ☐
- e ☐
- d ☐
- m ☐
- h ☐

78
- p ☐
- t ☐
- w ☐
- b ☐
- d ☐

79
- k ☐
- t ☐
- d ☐
- s ☐
- r ☐

80
- f ☐
- d ☐
- t ☐
- p ☐
- y ☐

11+VR-3   **END OF TEST**

Practice Paper 2

Verbal Reasoning

Read the following carefully:

1. **Do not open or turn over the page in this booklet until you are told to do so.**

2. This is a multiple-choice test in which you have to mark your answer to each question on the separate answer sheet.

3. The test contains a number of different types of question. Each question type starts with an explanation of what to do, usually followed by a worked example with the answer marked on the answer sheet.

4. Some questions require more than one answer to be marked. Read the instructions to each question carefully.

5. Draw a firm line clearly through the rectangle next to your answer like this ⬌. If you make a mistake, rub it out as completely as you can and put in your new answer.

6. Be sure to keep your place on the answer sheet. Mark your answer in the box that has the same number as the question.

7. You may not be able to finish all the questions, but try to do as many as you can. If you cannot do a question, **do not waste time on it but go on to the next**. If you are not sure of an answer, choose the one you think is best.

8. You may do any rough working on a separate sheet of paper.

9. **Work as quickly and as carefully as you can.**

10. You will have **50 minutes** to do the test.

In these questions, the **same** letter must fit into **both** sets of brackets, to complete the word in front of the brackets and begin the word after the brackets.
Find this letter and mark it on the answer sheet.

Example   mea [?] able   si [?] op

        A p   **B** n   **C** f   **D** t   **E** c

Answer   **t** (The four words are **meat**, **table**, **sit**, **top**.)

1   dis [?] urt   muc [?] ole

        A p   **B** h   **C** e   **D** s   **E** k

2   sof [?] in   bea [?] rap

        A d   **B** a   **C** t   **D** b   **E** w

3   ra [?] ain   fo [?] oat

        A t   **B** n   **C** g   **D** s   **E** p

4   tra [?] awn   bu [?] ellow

        A p   **B** d   **C** b   **D** s   **E** y

5   ea [?] an   sor [?] une

        A c   **B** y   **C** t   **D** d   **E** g

6   lin [?] itten   ran [?] ite

        A c   **B** m   **C** s   **D** n   **E** k

In these questions, the three numbers in **each** group are related in the **same** way.
Find the number that completes the last group and mark it on the answer sheet.

Example   (3 [6] 9)   (2 [4] 6)   (4 [?] 12)

A 3   **B** 4   **C** 6   **D** 8   **E** 10

Answer   **8**

7   (23 [91] 68)   (59 [93] 34)   (67 [?] 19)

A 83   **B** 84   **C** 85   **D** 86   **E** 87

8   (37 [54] 91)   (48 [34] 82)   (56 [?] 73)

A 17   **B** 21   **C** 34   **D** 39   **E** 41

9   (48 [37] 26)   (55 [38] 21)   (39 [?] 43)

A 29   **B** 35   **C** 37   **D** 38   **E** 41

10   (8 [55] 39)   (11 [35] 13)   (14 [?] 21)

A 8   **B** 35   **C** 39   **D** 47   **E** 49

11   (8 [3] 13)   (7 [6] 15)   (9 [?] 19)

A 7   **B** 8   **C** 9   **D** 11   **E** 12

12   (27 [55] 29)   (38 [88] 51)   (45 [?] 17)

A 59   **B** 60   **C** 61   **D** 62   **E** 63

In these questions, find **two** words, **one** from each group, that together make **one** correctly spelt word, without changing the order of the letters. The word from the first group always comes first. Mark **both** words on the answer sheet.

Example   (out   by   open)   (bite   like   side)

                  A out   **X** bite
                  B by   **Y** like
                  C open   **Z** side

Answer   **out   side**

13   (in   rain   hover)   (coat   fell   croft)

                  A in   **X** coat
                  B rain   **Y** fell
                  C hover   **Z** croft

14   (door   bad   had)   (lock   dock   ship)

                  A door   **X** lock
                  B bad   **Y** dock
                  C had   **Z** ship

15   (rope   hope   car)   (sat   tie   less)

                  A rope   **X** sat
                  B hope   **Y** tie
                  C car   **Z** less

16   (in   out   temp)   (late   down   slide)

    A in   **X** late
    B out   **Y** down
    C temp   **Z** slide

17   (ape   reap   grape)   (pear   wine   ate)

    A ape   **X** pear
    B reap   **Y** wine
    C grape   **Z** ate

18   (combine   share   do)   (state   nation   red)

    A combine   **X** state
    B share   **Y** nation
    C do   **Z** red

In these questions, three of the five words are related in some way.
Find the **two** words that do **not** go with these three and mark them **both** on the answer sheet.

Example   black   mouse   red   green   hut

A black   B mouse   C red   D green   E hut

Answer   **mouse   hut**

19   mug   china   cup   pottery   beaker

A mug   B china   C cup   D pottery   E beaker

20   handle   hammer   chisel   hand   saw

A handle   B hammer   C chisel   D hand   E saw

21   taste   sweet   touch   soft   see

A taste   B sweet   C touch   D soft   E see

22   river   stream   pour   tip   brook

A river   B stream   C pour   D tip   E brook

23   eyes   ears   arms   nose   legs

A eyes   B ears   C arms   D nose   E legs

24   around   long   tall   wide   across

A around   B long   C tall   D wide   E across

Read the following information, then find the correct answer to the question and mark its letter on the answer sheet.

25

David, Julie and Lee have to score at least 80% in a test in order to join the Science Club.

Julie scored 72%.

Both David and Lee scored higher than Julie.

If these statements are true, only one of the sentences below **must** be true.

Which one?

A   David and Lee passed the test.
B   Julie couldn't join the Science Club.
C   David and Lee couldn't join the Science Club.
D   Lee scored more than David.
E   David scored more than Lee.

In these questions, the three words in the second group should go together in the **same way** as the three in the first group.

Find the word that is missing in the second group and mark it on the answer sheet.

Example   (man [mat] tip)   (bug [?] dew)

A bud   B beg   C dug   D bed   E wed

Answer   **bud**

26

(show [hose] user)   (when [?] cart)

A tear   B hear   C went   D race   E hare

27

(bread [drips] clips)   (heart [?] prams)

A tears   B steam   C pears   D meats   E teams

28 (slide [dial] slave)   (spend [?] prank)

    A pear   **B** nape   **C** dear   **D** pans   **E** near

29 (sleep [plume] plums)   (print [?] claim)

    A trial   **B** trail   **C** train   **D** paint   **E** plain

30 (spike [kick] clock)   (jeans [?] mouse)

    A mean   **B** name   **C** same   **D** nose   **E** sane

31 (split [time] meant)   (thief [?] elbow)

    A flee   **B** blow   **C** heel   **D** blew   **E** feel

---

A B C D E F G H I J K L M N O P Q R S T U V W X Y Z

The alphabet is here to help you with these questions.
Find the next pair of letters in the series and mark it on the answer sheet.

Example   CQ   DQ   EP   FP   [?]

    A GP   **B** GO   **C** HO   **D** GR   **E** GQ

Answer   **GO**

32 EA   AC   JF   FH   OK   [?]

    A KM   **B** KO   **C** MO   **D** OM   **E** KN

33 BD CC CE DD DF EE [?]

    A EG   **B** EF   **C** FG   **D** FF   **E** FH

34 PO PR LK LN HG [?]

    A JG   **B** HI   **C** JH   **D** HK   **E** HJ

35 BC YX DE WV FG UT HI [?]

    A SR   **B** JK   **C** RQ   **D** RS   **E** IJ

36 QU RT SW TV UY [?]

    A WX   **B** WY   **C** VW   **D** VX   **E** WV

37 ZW WU UR RP PM [?]

    A MK   **B** PR   **C** MJ   **D** PS   **E** ML

In these sentences, the word in capitals has had three letters next to each other taken out.
These three letters will make one correctly spelt word without changing their order.
The sentence that you make must make sense.
Mark the correct three-letter word on the answer sheet.

Example   The cat scratched him with his **CS**.

A LAD   B LAW   C HAD   D RAW   E RED

Answer   **LAW** (The word in capitals is **CLAWS**.)

38   She **CED** the dog to follow her.

A ALL   B RYE   C ALE   D AWL   E HAS

39   The girl's behaviour **APLED** her teacher.

A ARE   B AWE   C ORE   D PAL   E PEA

40   He injured his **SE** in the accident.

A ELF   B PIT   C PIN   D CAN   E TON

41   They climbed the **SPEST** hill.

A TOP   B ARK   C ART   D TEE   E TEA

42   **FS** are very troublesome in summer.

A LOW   B LIE   C LAY   D RAG   E RAY

43   The two boys were fishing for **HS**.

A ACE   B EEL   C ALL   D OWE   E OUR

In these questions, one letter can be moved from the first word to the second word to make two new words.

The letters must **not** otherwise be rearranged and **both** new words must make sense.

Find the letter that moves and mark it on the answer sheet.

Example   pound   or

A p   B o   C u   D n   E d

Answer   **u** (The two new words are **pond** and **our**.)

44   joint   rim

A j   B o   C i   D n   E t

45   halve   bride

A h   B a   C l   D v   E e

46   brain   mad

A b   B r   C a   D i   E n

47   drink   boy

A d   B r   C i   D n   E k

48   chain   rot

A c   B h   C a   D i   E n

49   horse   tea

A h   B o   C r   D s   E e

In these questions, letters stand for numbers.

Work out the answer to each sum, then find its letter and mark it on the answer sheet.

Example   If A = 1, B = 2, C = 3, D = 6, E = 8,
what is the answer to this sum **written as a letter**?

A + B + C = [?]

A A   **B** B   **C** C   **D** D   **E** E

Answer   **D**

50   If A = 2, B = 10, C = 12, D = 18, E = 20,
what is the answer to this sum **written as a letter**?

C + D – E = [?]

A A   **B** B   **C** C   **D** D   **E** E

51   If A = 3, B = 6, C = 5, D = 2, E = 15,
what is the answer to this sum **written as a letter**?

B × C ÷ D = [?]

A A   **B** B   **C** C   **D** D   **E** E

52   If A = 3, B = 4, C = 6, D = 9, E = 18,
what is the answer to this sum **written as a letter**?

E × A ÷ D = [?]

A A   **B** B   **C** C   **D** D   **E** E

53 If A = 9, B = 6, C = 4, D = 24, E = 3,
what is the answer to this sum **written as a letter**?

$E \times C - A = [\,?\,]$

A A   **B** B   **C** C   **D** D   **E** E

54 If A = 9, B = 5, C = 45, D = 3, E = 1,
what is the answer to this sum **written as a letter**?

$D \times D \times B \div E = [\,?\,]$

A A   **B** B   **C** C   **D** D   **E** E

55 If A = 44, B = 11, C = 14, D = 22, E = 2,
what is the answer to this sum **written as a letter**?

$A \div B \times E + C = [\,?\,]$

A A   **B** B   **C** C   **D** D   **E** E

Read the following information, then find the correct answer to the question and mark its letter on the answer sheet.

56 David, Gemma, Jane, John and Maria are 12, 11, 10, 10 and 9 years old, but not in that order.
David is 2 years younger than John.
Gemma is 2 years younger than Jane.
Maria is older than David.

Who are the twins?

A David and Maria
B John and Jane
C Gemma and David
D Maria and Gemma
E John and Maria

In these questions, find the **two** words, **one** from each group, that will complete the sentence in the best way. Mark **both** words on the answer sheet.

Example   **Big** is to (small orange colour) as **wide** is to (apple red narrow).

A small   X apple

B orange   Y red

C colour   Z narrow

Answer   **small   narrow**

57   **Book** is to (library leaf tree) as **money** is to (paper bank pig).

A library   X paper

B leaf   Y bank

C tree   Z pig

58   **Early** is to (dawn late hour) as **stop** is to (bus queue start).

A dawn   X bus

B late   Y queue

C hour   Z start

59   **Shoes** are to (mouth feet month) as **gloves** are to (eyes hands time).

A mouth   X eyes

B feet   Y hands

C month   Z time

60 **Was** is to (is will not) as **saw** is to (hammer lake see).

A is   X hammer

B will   Y lake

C not   Z see

61 **Wind** is to (turn hurricane tree) as **rain** is to (downpour umbrella queen).

A turn   X downpour

B hurricane   Y umbrella

C tree   Z queen

62 **Assist** is to (help stock block) as **hinder** is to (falter fail delay).

A help   X falter

B stock   Y fail

C block   Z delay

A B C D E F G H I J K L M N O P Q R S T U V W X Y Z

The alphabet is here to help you with these questions.
Find the letters that will complete the sentence in the best way and mark the correct answer on the answer sheet.

Example   **AB** is to **CD** as **PQ** is to [?]

        A RT   **B** SR   **C** ST   **D** RS   **E** QR

Answer   **RS**

63
DE is to **FG** as **VW** is to [?]

        A HI   **B** MN   **C** XY   **D** YZ   **E** TU

64
ZX is to **VT** as **RP** is to [?]

        A ML   **B** ON   **C** KJ   **D** LK   **E** NL

65
AC is to **EG** as **SU** is to [?]

        A IK   **B** OQ   **C** UW   **D** XZ   **E** WY

66
BC is to **EF** as **HI** is to [?]

        A FG   **B** IJ   **C** KL   **D** NO   **E** QR

67
ZA is to **YB** as **XC** is to [?]

        A TE   **B** UE   **C** WD   **D** WE   **E** VG

68
AB is to **YZ** as **CD** is to [?]

        A KL   **B** EF   **C** XY   **D** WX   **E** RS

In these questions, find **two** words, **one** from each group, that are **closest in meaning**.
Mark **both** words on the answer sheet.

Example   (office   shop   start)   (work   begin   end)

A office   X work
B shop   Y begin
C start   Z end

Answer   **start   begin**

69   (little   pretty   cuddle)   (small   sweet   nice)

A little   X small
B pretty   Y sweet
C cuddle   Z nice

70   (idea   error   accurate)   (mistake   joke   fool)

A idea   X mistake
B error   Y joke
C accurate   Z fool

71   (bib   cot   rattle)   (sleep   baby   cradle)

A bib   X sleep
B cot   Y baby
C rattle   Z cradle

72   (quick   slow   idle)   (rapid   race   arena)

A quick   X rapid
B slow   Y race
C idle   Z arena

73

(bread butter eat)   (peas dinner feed)

A bread   X peas
B butter   Y dinner
C eat   Z feed

74

(high above apex)   (over inside under)

A high   X over
B above   Y inside
C apex   Z under

Three of these four words are given in code.

The codes are **not** written in the same order as the words and one code is missing.

SODA   TONE   EATS   TEND

1937   7469   3481

For these questions, mark the correct answer on the answer sheet.

75

Find the word that has the number code **8116**.

A NEED   B SOOT   C SEED   D TOON   E SOON

76

Find the word that has the number code **8431**.

A DOTE   B DATE   C NODE   D NOSE   E NOTE

77

Find the code for the word **DENT**.

A 6137   B 3467   C 7384   D 6183   E 7183

Three of these four words are given in code.

The codes are **not** written in the same order as the words and one code is missing.

PORT   TRAP   ROTA   PART

3421   2315   5432

For these questions, mark the correct answer on the answer sheet.

78   Find the code for the word **PART**.

A 3145   B 5132   C 5432   D 2135   E 2315

79   Find the code for the word **PROP**.

A 5435   B 2312   C 2412   D 2342   E 5345

80   Find the code for the word **ROOT**.

A 2113   B 3445   C 3442   D 2334   E 1334

Published by GL Assessment, 1st Floor, Vantage London, Great West Road, Brentford TW8 9AG.

Designed and typeset by Peter Francis.

Code 6801 031
1(11.18) PF

Practice Paper 1

Verbal Reasoning

Read the following carefully:

1. **Do not open or turn over the page in this booklet until you are told to do so.**

2. This is a multiple-choice test in which you have to mark your answer to each question on the separate answer sheet.

3. The test contains a number of different types of question. Each question type starts with an explanation of what to do, usually followed by a worked example with the answer marked on the answer sheet.

4. Some questions require more than one answer to be marked. Read the instructions to each question carefully.

5. Draw a firm line clearly through the rectangle next to your answer like this ⊟. If you make a mistake, rub it out as completely as you can and put in your new answer.

6. Be sure to keep your place on the answer sheet. Mark your answer in the box that has the same number as the question.

7. You may not be able to finish all the questions, but try to do as many as you can. If you cannot do a question, **do not waste time on it but go on to the next**. If you are not sure of an answer, choose the one you think is best.

8. You may do any rough working on a separate sheet of paper.

9. **Work as quickly and as carefully as you can.**

10. You will have **50 minutes** to do the test.

In these sentences, a word of **four letters** is hidden at the **end** of one word and the **beginning** of the next word.

Find the pair of words that contains the hidden word and mark this answer on the answer sheet.

Example   The film ended happily after all.

 A   The film

 B   film ended

 C   ended happily

 D   happily after

 E   after all.

Answer   **film ended** (The hidden word is **mend**.)

1   They saw that all the cake was gone.

 A   They saw

 B   saw that

 C   that all

 D   all the

 E   the cake

2   This item is out of stock.

 A   This item

 B   item is

 C   is out

 D   out of

 E   of stock.

3 Posters were stuck on the bedroom wall.

    A Posters were

    B were stuck

    C stuck on

    D on the

    E the bedroom

4 School began later during winter months.

    A School began

    B began later

    C later during

    D during winter

    E winter months.

5 Cats have better eyesight than dogs.

    A Cats have

    B have better

    C better eyesight

    D eyesight than

    E than dogs.

6 Wasps fly in through open windows.

    A Wasps fly

    B fly in

    C in through

    D through open

    E open windows.

In these questions, letters stand for numbers.

Work out the answer to each sum, then find its letter and mark it on the answer sheet.

Example   If A = 1, B = 2, C = 3, D = 6, E = 8,
what is the answer to this sum **written as a letter**?

A + B + C = [?]

A A   **B** B   **C** C   **D** D   **E** E

Answer   **D**

7   If A = 5, B = 7, C = 8, D = 9, E = 10,
what is the answer to this sum **written as a letter**?

B + C − E = [?]

A A   **B** B   **C** C   **D** D   **E** E

8   If A = 4, B = 6, C = 12, D = 18, E = 24,
what is the answer to this sum **written as a letter**?

A × C − E = [?]

A A   **B** B   **C** C   **D** D   **E** E

9   If A = 2, B = 3, C = 5, D = 10, E = 11,
what is the answer to this sum **written as a letter**?

A × B + C = [?]

A A   **B** B   **C** C   **D** D   **E** E

10 If A = 1, B = 2, C = 4, D = 8, E = 12,
what is the answer to this sum **written as a letter**?

E – D – B = [?]

  A A   **B** B   **C** C   **D** D   **E** E

11 If A = 10, B = 20, C = 30, D = 40, E = 50,
what is the answer to this sum **written as a letter**?

D ÷ B × A = [?]

  A A   **B** B   **C** C   **D** D   **E** E

12 If A = 12, B = 48, C = 84, D = 2, E = 6,
what is the answer to this sum **written as a letter**?

D × E × D + A + B = [?]

  A A   **B** B   **C** C   **D** D   **E** E

In these questions, one letter can be moved from the first word to the second word to make two new words.
The letters must **not** otherwise be rearranged and **both** new words must make sense.
Find the letter that moves and mark it on the answer sheet.

Example   pound   or

          A p   **B** o   **C** u   **D** n   **E** d

Answer   u (The two new words are **pond** and **our**.)

13   could   by

          A c   **B** o   **C** u   **D** l   **E** d

14 float   man

A f   B l   C o   D a   E t

15 stick   do

A s   B t   C i   D c   E k

16 grain   fir

A g   B r   C a   D i   E n

17 mince   lap

A m   B i   C n   D c   E e

18 reach   cow

A r   B e   C a   D c   E h

In these questions, find the **two** words, **one** from each group, that will complete the sentence in the best way. Mark **both** words on the answer sheet.

Example   **Big** is to (small   orange   colour) as **wide** is to (apple   red   narrow).

   A small   X apple
   B orange   Y red
   C colour   Z narrow

Answer   **small   narrow**

19   **Scales** are to (fins   pounds   weight) as **ruler** is to (tail   length   ounces).

   A fins   X tail
   B pounds   Y length
   C weight   Z ounces

20   **Thief** is to (take   crime   money) as **donor** is to (give   victim   blood).

   A take   X give
   B crime   Y victim
   C money   Z blood

21   **Valley** is to (below   country   green) as **mountain** is to (steep   above   jagged).

   A below   X steep
   B country   Y above
   C green   Z jagged

22   **Belt** is to (leather   buckle   laces) as **shirt** is to (collar   trousers   waistcoat).

   A leather   X collar
   B buckle   Y trousers
   C laces   Z waistcoat

23   **Jump** is to (high   walk   up) as **crouch** is to (down   move   hunch).

   A high   X down
   B walk   Y move
   C up   Z hunch

24   **Strong** is to (weak   great   lift) as **bold** is to (carry   timid   grand).

   A weak   X carry
   B great   Y timid
   C lift   Z grand

Read the following information, then find the correct answer to the question and mark it on the answer sheet.

25   Katie, Adam, Lucy, Ranjit and Mark all wear school uniform.
   Katie, Adam and Ranjit wear ties.
   Ranjit wears a shirt.
   Mark hates the uniform but wears a shirt and tie.
   Lucy and Katie wear jumpers.
   Adam wears a shirt but no jumper.

   Who wears the fewest items of uniform?

   A Katie   B Adam   C Lucy   D Ranjit   E Mark

In these questions, the three words in the second group should go together in the **same way** as the three in the first group.

Find the word that is missing in the second group and mark it on the answer sheet.

Example   (man [mat] tip)   (bug [?] dew)

A bud   B beg   C dug   D bed   E wed

Answer   **bud**

26   (spit [tip] past)   (sham [?] tend)

A ham   B hat   C mad   D sat   E mat

27   (trawl [water] lever)   (stock [?] fasts)

A casts   B tasks   C stack   D facts   E costs

28   (trout [roof] frost)   (spare [?] hotel)

A that   B real   C path   D reap   E hats

29   (tour [tear] reap)   (lead [?] rent)

A rend   B lend   C lent   D rate   E land

30   (rover [roar] board)   (flume [?] tails)

A lets   B fame   C mail   D flea   E fail

31   (alter [leer] pearl)   (chair [?] plate)

A hair   B hill   C hail   D halt   E hilt

In these sentences, the word in capitals has had three letters next to each other taken out.
These three letters will make one correctly-spelt word without changing their order.
The sentence that you make must make sense.
Mark the correct three-letter word on the answer sheet.

Example   The cat scratched him with his **CS**.

A LAD   B LAW   C HAD   D RAW   E RED

Answer   **LAW** (The word in capitals is **CLAWS**.)

32   It would be useful to take a **SE** sweatshirt.

A HAM   B HOP   C LAP   D PAR   E TAN

33   What is the **PR** of that?

A EAT   B ANT   C ICE   D ALL   E IMP

34   They were asked to **AD** their mistakes.

A MAN   B WIN   C MEN   D MEW   E WAY

35   The **FGE** is broken.

A RUN   B AND   C LID   D ASK   E RID

36   We liked the **MON** at the zoo.

A KEY   B CAR   C PIN   D SET   E ROD

37   The mist in the valley looked like **SM** rising.

A PAL   B OAK   C TEA   D ALE   E TAR

A B C D E F G H I J K L M N O P Q R S T U V W X Y Z

The alphabet is here to help you with these questions.

Find the letters that will complete the sentence in the best way and mark the correct answer on the answer sheet.

Example   **AB** is to **CD** as **PQ** is to [?]

             A RT   **B** SR   **C** ST   **D** RS   **E** QR

Answer   **RS**

38   **CX** is to **DW** as **HS** is to [?]

             A IS   **B** IT   **C** GT   **D** IR   **E** JQ

39   **BE** is to **GJ** as **CF** is to [?]

             A HK   **B** GJ   **C** HL   **D** FI   **E** GD

40   **AC** is to **BF** as **FH** is to [?]

             A GK   **B** GI   **C** HL   **D** FJ   **E** FK

41   **ZX** is to **AC** as **VT** is to [?]

             A GE   **B** DF   **C** EG   **D** GI   **E** CE

42   **VW** is to **RS** as **KL** is to [?]

             A HI   **B** HG   **C** IJ   **D** GH   **E** FG

43   **JK** is to **HL** as **PS** is to [?]

             A MT   **B** NQ   **C** NT   **D** QT   **E** OT

In these questions, find **two** words, **one** from each group, that are **closest in meaning**. Mark **both** words on the answer sheet.

Example   (office   shop   start)   (work   begin   end)

        A office   **X** work

        B shop   **Y** begin

        C start   **Z** end

Answer   **start   begin**

44   (game   trick   harm)   (play   hurt   chess)

        A game   **X** play

        B trick   **Y** hurt

        C harm   **Z** chess

45   (liquid   bend   soften)   (solid   set   melt)

        A liquid   **X** solid

        B bend   **Y** set

        C soften   **Z** melt

46   (sad   skilful   happy)   (concerned   able   lucky)

        A sad   **X** concerned

        B skilful   **Y** able

        C happy   **Z** lucky

47   (answer   echo   pretend)   (hollow   call   repeat)

        A answer   **X** hollow

        B echo   **Y** call

        C pretend   **Z** repeat

48   (raise   level   step)   (high   elevate   lower)

   A raise   X high
   B level   Y elevate
   C step   Z lower

49   (flight   customer   collect)   (client   tourist   expensive)

   A flight   X client
   B customer   Y tourist
   C collect   Z expensive

In these questions, find the number that continues the series in the most sensible way and mark it on the answer sheet.

Example   2   4   6   8   [?]

            A 16   B 11   C 10   D 9   E 12

Answer   **10**

50   7   9   13   19   27   [?]

            A 36   B 37   C 33   D 39   E 35

51   4   7   13   25   [?]

            A 43   B 35   C 49   D 51   E 37

52   2   4   12   48   [?]

            A 234   B 240   C 192   D 196   E 220

53

34   41   49   43   50   58   52   59   [?]

A 53   B 66   C 51   D 67   E 54

54

13   12   17   15   21   18   [?]

A 17   B 21   C 22   D 24   E 25

55

2   6   14   30   [?]

A 60   B 46   C 44   D 62   E 38

Read the following information, then find the correct answer to the question and mark its letter on the answer sheet.

56

Natalie, Michelle and Anthony have to be at school by 8.45 am.
Michelle is never late for school.
On Monday, Anthony was late for school.

If these statements are true, only one of the sentences below **must** be true.

Which one?

A Natalie is sometimes late for school.
B Anthony sometimes arrives after Michelle.
C Natalie sometimes arrives after Michelle.
D Anthony always arrives after Michelle.
E Natalie is never late for school.

In these questions, find **two** words, **one** from each group, that together make **one** correctly spelt word, without changing the order of the letters. The word from the first group always comes first. Mark **both** words on the answer sheet.

Example   (out   by   open)   (bite   like   side)

  A out   X bite
  B by   Y like
  C open   Z side

Answer   **out   side**

57   (fast   have   hope)   (like   ping   less)

  A fast   X like
  B have   Y ping
  C hope   Z less

58   (ball   table   data)   (bat   base   basket)

  A ball   X bat
  B table   Y base
  C data   Z basket

59   (pass   time   over)   (tall   by   take)

  A pass   X tall
  B time   Y by
  C over   Z take

60 (perm   with   look)   (at   on   it)

        A perm   **X** at
        B with   **Y** on
        C look   **Z** it

61 (imp   old   act)   (age   in   or)

        A imp   **X** age
        B old   **Y** in
        C act   **Z** or

62 (he   lie   lost)   (low   able   art)

        A he   **X** low
        B lie   **Y** able
        C lost   **Z** art

In these questions, there are two pairs of words.
Only one of the five possible answers will go equally well with **both** of these pairs.
Mark it on the answer sheet.

Example   (world   globe)   (soil   ground)

        A ball   **B** dirt   **C** plant   **D** earth   **E** universe

Answer   **earth**

63 (aroma   fragrance)   (track   trail)

        A path   **B** scent   **C** perfume   **D** way   **E** odour

64

(litter   trash)   (misuse   squander)

A corrupt   **B** break   **C** rubbish   **D** scrap   **E** waste

65

(apparent   evident)   (simple   bare)

A unmistakable   **B** unornamented   **C** unpatterned   **D** plain   **E** obvious

66

(remaining   unfinished)   (excellent   superior)

A outstanding   **B** extra   **C** senior   **D** surplus   **E** prime

67

(command   tell)   (arrange   position)

A ranked   **B** instruct   **C** demand   **D** tidy   **E** order

68

(sort   type)   (gentle   friendly)

A class   **B** pleasant   **C** variety   **D** kind   **E** nice

In these questions, three of the five words are related in some way.
Find the **two** words that do not go with these three and mark them **both** on the answer sheet.

Example   black   mouse   red   green   hut

        A black   **B** mouse   **C** red   **D** green   **E** hut

Answer   **mouse   hut**

69   ship   train   canal   tarmac   bus

        A ship   **B** train   **C** canal   **D** tarmac   **E** bus

70   carpet   curtain   blanket   pillow   sheet

        A carpet   **B** curtain   **C** blanket   **D** pillow   **E** sheet

71   milk   desert   camel   zebra   cat

        A milk   **B** desert   **C** camel   **D** zebra   **E** cat

72   tennis   racket   rounders   stadium   football

        A tennis   **B** racket   **C** rounders   **D** stadium   **E** football

73   spoon   rake   fork   wheel   spade

        A spoon   **B** rake   **C** fork   **D** wheel   **E** spade

74   beret   head   cap   bonnet   car

        A beret   **B** head   **C** cap   **D** bonnet   **E** car

A B C D E F G H I J K L M N O P Q R S T U V W X Y Z

The alphabet is here to help you with these questions.
You need to work out a **different** code for **each** question.
Choose the correct answer and mark it on the answer sheet.

Example   If the code for **FOOT** is **ENNS**, what is the code for **TOE**?

A STU   B SND   C UPF   D SRQ   E SNE

Answer   **SND**

75   If the code for **CALF** is **FDOI**, what is the code for **LAMB**?

A NCPE   B ODPE   C IXJY   D NCOD   E ODQF

76   If the code for **CRATE** is **YNWPA**, what is the code for **BOX**?

A FSB   B XJS   C FTA   D YLU   E XKT

77   If the code for **ORANGE** is **RUDQJH**, what does **SLQN** mean?

A PEAR   B PLUM   C PINK   D PALE   E PUCE

78   If the code for **NETBALL** is **PCVZCJN**, what is the code for **FOOTBALL**?

A HMQRDYNJ   B HQQVZCJN   C GPPUZCJN   D HQQVDCNN   E GNPSZCJN

79   If the code for **TREE** is **QOBB**, what does **DOXPP** mean?

A BRASS   B GRASS   C GREEN   D GROWS   E STAFF

80   If the code for **PIANO** is **QKDRT**, what is the code for **VIOLIN**?

A WJPMJO   B WHPKJO   C WHNKHM   D WKPNJP   E WKRPNT

Published by GL Assessment, 1st Floor, Vantage London, Great West Road, Brentford TW8 9AG.

Designed and typeset by Peter Francis.

Code 6801 030
1(11.18) PF

Practice Paper 3

Verbal Reasoning

Read the following carefully:

1. **Do not open or turn over the page in this booklet until you are told to do so.**
2. This is a multiple-choice test in which you have to mark your answer to each question on the separate answer sheet.
3. The test contains a number of different types of question. Each question type starts with an explanation of what to do, usually followed by a worked example with the answer marked on the answer sheet.
4. Some questions require more than one answer to be marked. Read the instructions to each question carefully.
5. Draw a firm line clearly through the rectangle next to your answer like this ▭. If you make a mistake, rub it out as completely as you can and put in your new answer.
6. Be sure to keep your place on the answer sheet. Mark your answer in the box that has the same number as the question.
7. You may not be able to finish all the questions, but try to do as many as you can. If you cannot do a question, **do not waste time on it but go on to the next**. If you are not sure of an answer, choose the one you think is best.
8. You may do any rough working on a separate sheet of paper.
9. **Work as quickly and as carefully as you can.**
10. You will have **50 minutes** to do the test.

In these sentences, a word of **four letters** is hidden at the **end** of one word and the **beginning** of the next word.

Find the pair of words that contains the hidden word and mark this answer on the answer sheet.

Example   The film ended happily after all.

        A The film

        B film ended

        C ended happily

        D happily after

        E after all.

Answer   **film ended** (The hidden word is **mend**.)

1   The girl ate the sponge cake.

        A The girl

        B girl ate

        C ate the

        D the sponge

        E sponge cake.

2   Soon they are all going on holiday.

        A Soon they

        B are all

        C all going

        D going on

        E on holiday.

3 Glass bottles should be kept upright.

A Glass bottles

B bottles should

C should be

D be kept

E kept upright.

4 We get ripe apples in October.

A We get

B get ripe

C ripe apples

D apples in

E in October.

5 My drink is hotter than yours.

A My drink

B drink is

C is hotter

D hotter than

E than yours.

6 He had hurt his knee badly.

A He had

B had hurt

C hurt his

D his knee

E knee badly.

In these questions, find the number that will complete the sum correctly and mark it on the answer sheet.

Example $3 + 5 = 6 + [\,?\,]$

A 1   B 2   C 3   D 4   E 5

Answer   **2**

7 $68 + 75 + 23 = 85 + [\,?\,]$

A 79   B 80   C 81   D 82   E 83

8 $33 \div 11 + 5 = 16 \div [\,?\,]$

A 2   B 3   C 4   D 6   E 8

9 $6 \times 9 = 5 \times [\,?\,] + 4$

A 7   B 8   C 9   D 10   E 11

10 $3 \times 9 + 8 = 5 \times [\,?\,]$

A 5   B 6   C 7   D 8   E 9

11 $100 \div 20 = 6 \times [\,?\,] - 7$

A 2   B 3   C 4   D 5   E 6

12 $4 \times 4 - 8 = [\,?\,] \div 4$

A 12   B 16   C 24   D 30   E 32

In these questions, find **two** words, **one** from each group, that are **closest in meaning**. Mark **both** words on the answer sheet.

Example   (office   shop   start)   (work   begin   end)

A office   X work
B shop   Y begin
C start   Z end

Answer   **start   begin**

13   (work   type   succeed)   (labour   plan   office)

A work   X labour
B type   Y plan
C succeed   Z office

14   (soup   fork   bowl)   (bread   dish   knife)

A soup   X bread
B fork   Y dish
C bowl   Z knife

15   (stone   sea   beach)   (hill   rock   grass)

A stone   X hill
B sea   Y rock
C beach   Z grass

16   (sand   bucket   water)   (garden   spade   pail)

A sand   X garden
B bucket   Y spade
C water   Z pail

17   (circus   funny   laugh)   (game   clown   witty)

        A circus   X game
        B funny   Y clown
        C laugh   Z witty

18   (flower   tree   leaf)   (spring   blossom   grass)

        A flower   X spring
        B tree   Y blossom
        C leaf   Z grass

In these questions, three of the five words are related in some way.
Find the **two** words that do **not** go with these three and mark them **both** on the answer sheet.

Example   black   mouse   red   green   hut

        A black   B mouse   C red   D green   E hut

Answer   **mouse   hut**

19   over   under   cricket   tennis   badminton

        A over   B under   C cricket   D tennis   E badminton

20   joy   laugh   cry   sad   scream

        A joy   B laugh   C cry   D sad   E scream

21   hat   feet   coat   head   shoes

        A hat   B feet   C coat   D head   E shoes

22 bathroom   kitchen   garden   bedroom   lawn

A bathroom   **B** kitchen   **C** garden   **D** bedroom   **E** lawn

23 lightning   thunder   hail   sleet   snow

A lightning   **B** thunder   **C** hail   **D** sleet   **E** snow

24 beneath   because   beware   behind   between

A beneath   **B** because   **C** beware   **D** behind   **E** between

---

Read the following information, then find the correct answer to the question and mark it on the answer sheet.

25 Malcolm, Mohammed, Beth, Sally and Robin all have pets.
Malcolm, Mohammed and Robin each have a dog.
Malcolm has a cat.
Sally loves horses but only has a rabbit and a snake.
Mohammed also has a snake.
Beth and Robin have a parrot each.

Who keeps the fewest pets?

A Malcolm
B Mohammed
C Beth
D Sally
E Robin

In these questions, the three words in the second group should go together in the **same way** as the three in the first group.

Find the word that is missing in the second group and mark it on the answer sheet.

Example   (man [mat] tip)   (bug [?] dew)

A bud   B beg   C dug   D bed   E wed

Answer   **bud**

26   (hour [ogre] gave)   (step [?] able)

A tale   B bale   C base   D tape   E peat

27   (hen [not] pot)   (eat [?] she)

A the   B tea   C sat   D set   E hat

28   (chain [hate] paste)   (blood [?] droop)

A lord   B door   C prod   D loop   E pool

29   (plead [date] enter)   (gloat [?] stile)

A tail   B tile   C last   D lost   E tale

30   (torch [chart] parts)   (trial [?] berth)

A reads   B laird   C deals   D alert   E leads

31   (weird [ware] azure)   (stoat [?] pleat)

A spot   B step   C stop   D eats   E spat

A B C D E F G H I J K L M N O P Q R S T U V W X Y Z

The alphabet is here to help you with these questions.
You need to work out a **different** code for **each** question.
Choose the correct answer and mark it on the answer sheet.

Example   If the code for **FOOT** is **ENNS**, what is the code for **TOE**?

A STU   B SND   C UPF   D SRQ   E SNE

Answer   **SND**

32   If the code for **CRY** is **FUB**, what does **ELQ** mean?

A HIT   B HOT   C HOG   D BIN   E BIT

33   If the code for **BLACK** is **DNCEM**, what is the code for **WHITE**?

A YJKVG   B UFGRC   C ZKLWH   D ZJKWG   E YJLVG

34   If the code for **LEOPARD** is **KFNQZSC**, what is the code for **CHEETAH**?

A BGDDSZG   B BIDFSBG   C DIFFUZI   D DGFDUZI   E EJGGVCJ

35   If the code for **SATSUMA** is **RBSTTNZ**, what does **RQQPTUR** mean?

A SAUSAGE   B FEEDING   C SPROUTS   D PUDDING   E LASAGNE

36   If the code for **FROG** is **GTRK**, what does **TRRX** mean?

A EELS   B SPOT   C POOL   D POND   E SOFT

37   If the code for **TRAIN** is **RSXJJ**, what is the code for **PASTE**?

A NYQSY   B NXPUB   C NBQUY   D RZVSI   E NBPUA

In these sentences, the word in capitals has had three letters next to each other taken out.
These three letters will make one correctly spelt word without changing their order.
The sentence that you make must make sense.
Mark the correct three-letter word on the answer sheet.

Example   The cat scratched him with his **CS**.

A LAD   B LAW   C HAD   D RAW   E RED

Answer   LAW (The word in capitals is **CLAWS**.)

38   She pulled her **SF** around her to keep warm.

A COT   B CAN   C TAR   D HAT   E CAR

39   John goes to **SCS** every Thursday.

A PAR   B COT   C OUT   D ARE   E OUR

40   They rode chestnut **MS** while on holiday.

A ATE   B AIR   C ARE   D OUT   E OWL

41   They kept the bottles in a **CE**.

A HAT   B HIM   C RIM   D RAT   E ROT

42   The girl was **HST** and owned up to what she had done.

A APE   B OWN   C ONE   D ARE   E WON

43   She hid it in the **FS** of her coat.

A RUN   B OLD   C OWL   D ROC   E AIR

In these questions, find **two** words, **one** from each group, that together make **one** correctly spelt word, without changing the order of the letters. The word from the first group always comes first. Mark **both** words on the answer sheet.

Example   (out by open)   (bite like side)

                    A out   **X** bite
                    B by   **Y** like
                    C open   **Z** side

Answer   **out   side**

44   (back four front)   (pane ground under)

                    A back   **X** pane
                    B four   **Y** ground
                    C front   **Z** under

45   (ear are under)   (grind were wear)

                    A ear   **X** grind
                    B are   **Y** were
                    C under   **Z** wear

46   (ever green red)   (house moor dye)

                    A ever   **X** house
                    B green   **Y** moor
                    C red   **Z** dye

47   (top in out)   (form shape shop)

         A top   **X** form

         B in   **Y** shape

         C out   **Z** shop

48   (win red bar)   (rose doe gain)

         A win   **X** rose

         B red   **Y** doe

         C bar   **Z** gain

49   (man boy say)   (fell age here)

         A man   **X** fell

         B boy   **Y** age

         C say   **Z** here

In these questions, find the number that continues the series in the most sensible way and mark it on the answer sheet.

Example   2   4   6   8   [?]

         A 16   **B** 11   **C** 10   **D** 9   **E** 12

Answer   **10**

50   3   6   12   24   [?]

         A 64   **B** 48   **C** 12   **D** 4   **E** 16

51

23   15   27   19   31   [?]

A 22   B 23   C 25   D 29   E 27

52

14   11   21   18   28   25   35   [?]

A 32   B 42   C 40   D 30   E 33

53

5   3   11   9   [?]

A 20   B 19   C 15   D 17   E 21

54

12   21   39   75   [?]

A 57   B 113   C 101   D 147   E 99

55

40   39   35   40   30   41   [?]

A 50   B 20   C 42   D 25   E 39

Read the following information, then find the correct answer to the question and mark its letter on the answer sheet.

56 Randeep, Kim and Jon go to the cinema every Friday.
The film always starts at 6.30 pm.
Jon is never more than 20 minutes early, and Randeep can be up to 10 minutes late.

If these statements are true, only one of the sentences below **must** be true.

Which one?

A   Kim is always on time.
B   Jon could arrive by 6 pm.
C   Randeep doesn't like the cinema much.
D   Randeep would always have arrived before 6.45 pm.
E   Jon and Kim always arrive early.

In these questions, find the **two** words, **one** from each group, that will complete the sentence in the best way. Mark **both** words on the answer sheet.

Example   **Big** is to (small   orange   colour) as **wide** is to (apple   red   narrow).

A small   X apple
B orange   Y red
C colour   Z narrow

Answer   **small   narrow**

57 **Leaf** is to (plant   green   live) as **blade** is to (knife   sharp   ice).

A plant   X knife
B green   Y sharp
C live   Z ice

58 **Aeroplane** is to (distant fly sky) as **submarine** is to (swim sea near).

A distant   X swim

B fly   Y sea

C sky   Z near

59 **Book** is to (writing novel paper) as **window** is to (door house glass).

A writing   X door

B novel   Y house

C paper   Z glass

60 **Selfish** is to (tight crab generous) as **cruel** is to (type kind child).

A tight   X type

B crab   Y kind

C generous Z child

61 **Fore** is to (ground front head) as **rear** is to (back leg air).

A ground   X back

B front   Y leg

C head   Z air

62 **May** is to (month might season) as **Friday** is to (end day Thursday).

A month   X end

B might   Y day

C season   Z Thursday

In these questions, one letter can be moved from the first word to the second word to make two new words.

The letters must **not** otherwise be rearranged and **both** new words must make sense.

Find the letter that moves and mark it on the answer sheet.

Example   pound   or

    A p   B o   C u   D n   E d

Answer   u (The two new words are **pond** and **our**.)

63   plant   pay

    A p   B l   C a   D n   E t

64   brush   cad

    A b   B r   C u   D s   E h

65   proven   give

    A p   B r   C o   D v   E n

66   cheap   grim

    A c   B h   C e   D a   E p

67   hostel   on

    A h   B o   C s   D t   E e

68   irate   clam

    A i   B r   C a   D t   E e

A B C D E F G H I J K L M N O P Q R S T U V W X Y Z

The alphabet is here to help you with these questions.

Find the letters that will complete the sentence in the best way and mark the correct answer on the answer sheet.

Example   **AB** is to **CD** as **PQ** is to [?]

          A RT   **B** SR   **C** ST   **D** RS   **E** QR

Answer   **RS**

69

HI is to **KL** as **NO** is to [?]

          A AB   **B** EF   **C** TU   **D** ST   **E** QR

70

ZY is to **XW** as **VU** is to [?]

          A NM   **B** PO   **C** RQ   **D** TS   **E** TR

71

CF is to **IL** as **OR** is to [?]

          A KJ   **B** ON   **C** UW   **D** UX   **E** XZ

72

ZW is to **TQ** as **NK** is to [?]

          A HG   **B** JH   **C** HE   **D** EB   **E** NL

73

CD is to **GH** as **KL** is to [?]

          A RS   **B** PQ   **C** NO   **D** OP   **E** ST

74

BH is to **WF** as **CD** is to [?]

          A YB   **B** XB   **C** YA   **D** XA   **E** AY

In these questions, the **same** letter must fit into **both** sets of brackets, to complete the word in front of the brackets and begin the word after the brackets.

Find this letter and mark it on the answer sheet.

Example   mea [?] able   si [?] op

       A p   **B** n   **C** f   **D** t   **E** c

Answer   **t** (The four words are **meat**, **table**, **sit**, **top**.)

75   poe [?] ean   fro [?] ile

       A t   **B** g   **C** l   **D** m   **E** b

76   ta [?] each   sna [?] art

       A t   **B** d   **C** m   **D** r   **E** p

77   bas [?] asy   fin [?] ating

       A s   **B** e   **C** d   **D** m   **E** h

78   cro [?] alk   pa [?] in

       A p   **B** t   **C** w   **D** b   **E** d

79   brea [?] ink   pin [?] now

       A k   **B** t   **C** d   **D** s   **E** r

80   sa [?] ear   ver [?] olk

       A f   **B** d   **C** t   **D** p   **E** y

ISBN 978-0-70872-761-4

9 780708 727614

Published by GL Assessment, 1st Floor, Vantage London, Great West Road, Brentford TW8 9AG.

Designed and typeset by Peter Francis.

Code 6801 032
1(11.18) PF